WORDS *of* HOPE *and* HEALING

THE
ANXIETY
of GRIEF

How *to* Understand,
Soothe, *and* Express your
Fears after *a* Loss

Alan D. Wolfelt, Ph.D.

Companion
PRESS

An imprint of the Center for Loss and Life Transition | Fort Collins, Colorado

Companion Press is an imprint of the Center for Loss and Life Transition, 3735 Broken Bow Road, Fort Collins, Colorado 80526.

28   27   26   25   24   23   6 5 4 3 2 1

ISBN: 978-1-61722-332-7

CONTENTS

WELCOME

"No one ever told me that grief felt so like fear."
— C.S. Lewis

Someone in your life has died, and you are grieving.

No doubt you have experienced many different emotions since the death. But if you are reading this particular book, you may especially be struggling with anxious thoughts and feelings.

Anxiety in grief is natural. It's natural because death and loss are naturally stressful. Like many emotions in grief, however, anxiety is also difficult and unpleasant. And if it's causing you to be overwhelmed by the demands of daily life, or if it's continuing at a high level for an extended period of time, it can be debilitating.

I wrote this little book to help you understand and soothe your anxiety in the aftermath of a painful loss. Even if you're grieving, you don't need to live in a constant state of anxiety. In fact, it's not good for your health. So we'll go over ways in which you can recognize, soothe, and help yourself with your anxiety whenever you need to.

Grief is normal. Anxiety in grief is normal. But even normal life experiences require effective responses. Developing skills to better befriend and calm your anxiety is part of your path forward.

PART ONE

UNDERSTANDING YOUR ANXIETY

"Grief is like the ocean; it comes on waves, ebbing and flowing. Sometimes the water is calm, and sometimes it is overwhelming. All we can do is learn to swim."

— Vicki Harrison

Understanding is the first step in navigating so many challenges in life. This includes the anxiety of grief. So let's begin by taking a look at the fundamentals of grief and anxiety.

WHAT IS GRIEF?

Grief is everything we think and feel inside of ourselves after a loss.

Grief is the single, collective term we use to describe the full range of thoughts, feelings, and behaviors we experience after a death.

If we think of grief as a basket, we can see that the basket holds all of our responses to a loss. Our shock and numbness go in the basket. Our sadness goes in the basket. Our anger goes in the basket. Our tears go in the basket. Our worries about the funeral, the effects this loss will have on others, and our future without the person who died go in the basket, too.

Grief is a big basket. It holds everything. And everything it holds is normal. There are no abnormal responses to loss.

In our lives, death itself is actually the abnormality. What I mean by that is that today, in our advanced cultures with long average lifespans, death is something most of us face relatively rarely. Death is also normal, of course, but its infrequency in our own personal circles makes it feel like the intruder. It is the unusual thing that comes along and knocks us off our feet.

And grief? Grief is how we learn to live through and beyond the shattering experience of the death of someone we love.

WHAT IS ANXIETY?

Anxiety is a normal response to stress. It is a form of fear.

You can think of anxiety as a warning signal that something may be going wrong. Often it cautions us about potential future harm. When we walk along a cliff, for example, our anxiety tells us not to get too close to the edge. If a tornado is approaching, our anxiety warns us to take cover. In these ways, our anxiety is not only ordinary, it's helpful—and even necessary to our continued survival.

Anxiety can show up in lots of ways. It includes stressful thoughts, but it also is felt in the body. On the next page, put a checkmark next to any of the anxiety symptoms you've been having.

- [ ] Feeling nervous, restless, agitated, or irritable
- [ ] Repetitive thoughts of worry about something bad that might happen, or replaying thoughts about bad things that have already happened
- [ ] Trouble sleeping
- [ ] Fatigue and/or weakness
- [ ] Difficulty concentrating, brain fog
- [ ] Being fidgety or jumpy, startling easily, trembling
- [ ] Bodily pains such as headaches, stomachaches, muscle pain, heartburn, tingling sensations
- [ ] Shortness of breath, racing heart, tightness of chest
- [ ] Repetitive behaviors, tics
- [ ] Avoiding certain places, people, and circumstances because they make you feel stressed
- [ ] Over-isolating yourself
- [ ] Fearing that you're going crazy

Anything else? Please add it to the list.

_____

_____

_____

Why is fear so common in grief, especially in the early months? There are a number of reasons fear and anxiety are often a big part of the grief experience.

1. The death of someone we love impacts our **sense of safety**, which arouses our bodies' fight, flight, or freeze systems. Stress chemicals flood our bloodstreams. Our minds and bodies are placed on high alert for the possibility of more danger. We'll be talking more about this evolutionary physical response soon.

2. A death often creates numerous **practical stressors**. In the first weeks and months, immediate family members and close friends have a lot to take care of. People must be notified and funerals planned. Many forms have to be completed. Financial matters must be tended to. Difficult conversations are required. All of these obligations are stressful and compound the natural biochemistry of fear.

3. Death naturally causes **existential fear**. It makes us worry about how or if we'll survive being shattered. We are forced to confront unanswerable questions about the meaning and purpose of life. We realize how vulnerable we are—and how vulnerable other loved ones who are still living may be. Life's cruelty and fleetingness are especially pronounced at this time, and that can feel scary.

The Anxiety of Grief

4. A **core relationship has been severed**. Our relationships often make us feel safe and secure in who we are as individuals. We have a place in our small world of close family and friends. When someone in our core group dies, we are forced to reconstruct our unique roles and ways of being within the group. In addition, our central relationships ground us as part of a family and a community. Our loved ones are our anchors and refuge in a stormy world. When one of our main anchors is no longer there to secure us, we tend to feel unmoored and adrift. That's frightening. The prospect of having to rebuild both our self-identity and sense of security can be overwhelming.

5. And finally, I have learned well in my four decades as a grief counselor and educator that after a significant loss, **we are often afraid to wholeheartedly grieve and mourn**. Why? Because our culture teaches us that what we need to do is get past the death and "move on."

   Grief is generally not acknowledged as the necessary, hurtful, long-lasting time of injury and convalescence that it is. The unwritten rules are:

   - Big feelings are often not welcome, especially in public or around others.

   - Any expression of pain should largely be private.

- The best way forward is to keep a stiff upper lip and remain in control.

So, having internalized these misconceptions, most of us see grief as a foe rather than a friend. We tend to distract ourselves from our own true feelings. We deny ourselves full expression. We're scared to lose control. We're afraid we're crazy. But the terrible irony is that in moving away from instead of toward our grief, we only compound our feelings of anxiety.

Avoiding authentic grief and mourning is like putting off any critical life task, hoping it will just go away. It won't. The difficulty is still there, and trying to ignore it only makes it worse. Deep down we know this, and so our anxiety over the loss and our suppressed feelings bubbles and builds.

It's no wonder fear and anxiety can be such a big part of grief. Acknowledging and working to understand the anxiety is the first step. The next is finding ways to soothe the anxiety. Building a well-stocked toolkit of effective soothing strategies will help you survive this time. And the final step is fully expressing the anxiety as well as all your thoughts and feelings in grief.

The Anxiety of Grief

MY ANXIETY

Have you been experiencing some of the symptoms on page 5?
How would you describe your own anxiety? Take a moment to jot
down, in your own words, what your anxiety in grief has been like
for you. To the extent that you understand the possible causes,
explain the reasons why you believe you are anxious. Also mention
any other factors besides the death that may be contributing to
your anxiety.

_____

_____

_____

_____

_____

_____

_____

_____

_____

_____

_____

_____

THE BIOCHEMISTRY OF FEAR

We have evolutionary biology to thank for some of the fear-based symptoms of early grief.

When we are under immediate threat, our ancient fight, flight, or freeze system kicks in. This is the biological wiring that evolved to keep us alive in dangerous situations. Here's a quick lesson:

Imagine I suddenly notice that a predator—a grizzly bear, say—is nearby and approaching me. My brain recognizes "Danger!" and activates my sympathetic nervous system and my adrenocortical system. This sets a cascade of physical responses in motion.

My sympathetic nervous system uses nerve pathways in my body to initiate reactions, while my adrenocortical system releases hormones through the bloodstream.

My brain's amygdalae, two small clusters of cells deep in my temporal lobes that are in charge of emotional processing, interpret what I am seeing as danger and instantly send a distress signal to my hypothalamus. My hypothalamus is my stress command center, in charge of my autonomic nervous system. It reaches out to my adrenal glands, which pump out epinephrine, a.k.a. adrenaline.

My heart rate increases, pushing blood to my muscles, heart, and other vital organs.

My breathing rate speeds up so I can take in more oxygen.

My digestion slows down or stops, because it's not necessary right now.

My blood vessels constrict to channel blood to my muscles.

My pupils dilate so I can see better.

My brain receives the extra oxygen and goes into hyper-alert status.

In short, my body prepares to either stay and fight, freeze in an attempt to "play dead," or run away.

After the initial surge of adrenaline subsides, if I am still seeing that scary grizzly bear, my hypothalamus activates what is known as the HPA (hypothalamic-pituitary-adrenal) axis. This second punch in the one-two punch stress response keeps my body in hyperalert mode.

My pituitary releases a hormone called adrenocorticotropic hormone, or ACTH, which travels to my adrenal glands, prompting them to release cortisol. Cortisol is also called "the stress hormone." It maintains my body's fluid balance and blood pressure and blocks non-essential bodily functions, such as reproductive drive, immunity, and growth.

All of this happens without my conscious awareness or permission. Instead, my body's reaction to danger is subconscious and primal.

The name that we use to describe what my body is feeling after I see the bear is "fear." I see danger, so I feel fear. In other words, fear is what it feels like in my body when my body's primal fight-or-flight-or-freeze system has been activated. For millennia, fear has kept human beings alive. When we are in true physical danger, it still does. You'd better believe that if I encounter a grizzly bear on my next hike in the northern Rocky Mountains, I'll be grateful for fear.

But now human societies and technologies have evolved to the point that in our daily lives we rarely experience imminent life-or-death situations. We most often experience fear after an incident that's scary and/or emotionally stressful. Death is scary and stressful emotionally. So death naturally causes fear.

IS YOUR ANXIETY DUE TO THE LOSS?

In grief, you may experience symptoms of anxiety and understand that they are clearly related to your loss. For example, you may be thinking about the loss a lot and feeling anxious in your body as you do so.

Or you might have been experiencing an anxiety symptom such as irritability without realizing that a) it's anxiety, and b) the loss was in fact a major contributor. Understanding all the ways in which anxiety can show up will help you recognize it when it affects you.

What's more, feelings are often multicausal. That is, it's common for them to be caused or heightened by multiple things. So it's very possible that your current struggles with anxiety are being triggered by other life circumstances in addition to the loss as well as any preexisting tendencies toward anxiety or depression. Regardless of the cause(s) of your anxiety, the suggestions in this book will help you learn to soothe and express it.

If it turns out that you need more assistance understanding your unique anxieties and ways to alleviate them, it will be helpful for you to see a grief counselor for consultation and follow-up sessions. A trained, compassionate counselor can help you take inventory of all your grief symptoms and wellness challenges, explore how the loss as well as other life circumstances fit into the picture, and create a plan to understand and help with your anxiety.

ANXIETY SERVES A PURPOSE

I strongly believe that all feelings in grief have a purpose.

Grief is the process that ushers us through the transition from life before the death to life after the death. This makes it normal and necessary. After all, what would the alternative to grief be? When someone dies, could we simply shrug our shoulders and continue on with our lives as if nothing had happened? Of course not! Where there is love, there is attachment. And whenever attachments are severed, there is grief.

If grief is necessary, so, too, are the thoughts and feelings that naturally arise in grief. They are, in essence, the "work" of grief. You may have heard the phrase "You need to feel it to heal it." It's true. It becomes our job to experience, understand, and express our thoughts and emotions as they come up. In grief, each new day brings a new mixture of thoughts and feelings. Certain emotions and ideas may continue for long stretches of time, but they also change. Some get stronger. Some fade. Some ebb and flow. Some take on new qualities and rationales.

Along the way, each grief feeling on any given day is there for a reason. If you're angry, for instance, you're probably feeling a sense of injustice and a lack of control. Exploring those feelings by mourning them—in other words, expressing them outside yourself—is part of your work on that day. Journaling, talking to a friend, praying or meditating, sharing with a counselor—these are ways to engage with and express your anger. If you're angry again tomorrow, you continue the hard work of mourning that feeling. As you've no doubt already learned, encountering your grief is a one-day-at-a-time process.

In general, the more actively you work with and express a

feeling, the more quickly and fully it will, over time, soften. Your mind and soul require this work in order to acknowledge and integrate the loss. They can't weave it into the tapestry of your life without the work of grief and mourning. And so, ultimately, healing in grief requires ongoing, active engagement with every prominent thought and feeling.

This includes fear and anxiety. Learning about all the reasons you are anxious is part of your grief work. You can think on it and journal about it. You can and should also talk to others about it. When it comes to reconciling grief, there is no substitute for the listening ears and compassionate empathy of our fellow human beings. We'll talk more about mourning your anxiety in Part Three.

NORMAL ANXIETY OR ANXIETY DISORDER?

As discussed, anxiety in grief arises for reasons that make sense. But when it becomes generalized and chronic, it's no longer serving its purpose. It's simply not healthy to feel anxious all or most of the time. If anxiety goes on intensely for too long, it can harm your health because the stress chemicals we talked about on pages 10 to 12 cause and worsen disease. Studies show that chronic anxiety weakens our immune systems, causes cardiovascular damage, leads to gastrointestinal trouble, accelerates aging, worsens memory and decision-making, and can cause clinical depression.

Anxiety can also get in the way of other mourning work that can help you integrate and move through your grief. It can throw up a roadblock that stalls and even intensifies grief. Earlier I suggested that mourners often feel anxious in part because they're denying, minimizing, and/or suppressing the expression of their normal and necessary grief. The corollary is also true: anxiety can prevent you from getting your grief back on a healthy track. It can be a vicious cycle that worsens over time.

So how do you know if your anxiety is normal grief anxiety or has become an anxiety disorder?

First, it's not black or white. Especially in early grief, it's quite common to experience a great deal of anxiety. I can think of nothing more naturally stressful— physically, cognitively, emotionally, socially, and spiritually—than the death of a loved one.

But if you're having trouble functioning day to day, especially if some months have passed since the death, or if you're having panic attacks at any time, it's essential to talk to your primary-care provider about your anxiety. Depending upon their recommendations, you may consider medication and/or therapy to help you calm your anxiety enough to restore a baseline level of functioning and enable you to engage with your grief in healthy ways.

Red flags for anxiety disorders may include:

- Not sleeping enough or too much
- Not eating enough or too much
- Being unable to care for yourself—bathing, basic hygiene, getting dressed, daily tasks of living
- Avoiding leaving the house or going places
- Avoiding driving, cooking, paying bills, and other necessary tasks
- Avoiding interacting with others
- Being unable to communicate with others
- Obsessive thinking or behaviors
- Experiencing debilitating phobias (such as fear of public places, enclosed spaces, transportation, etc.)
- Panic attacks
- Severe depression (clinical anxiety and depression often go hand-in-hand)

Panic attacks are sudden episodes of severe fear and anxiety. Panic happens when the body's fight, flight, or freeze system goes into high alert, causing symptoms such as:

- Racing heart
- Sweating
- Chest pain
- Trembling, shaking

- Strong feelings of imminent danger or impending doom
- Strong feelings of being unable to survive
- Strong feelings of being out of control

Panic attacks are scary and debilitating. However certain medications can bring you relief, as can counseling.

Again, if you are suffering panic attacks or think you may have an anxiety disorder, make an appointment with your primary-care provider without delay. They will help you find ways to calm disabling levels of anxiety so that you are once again able to function in your daily life and engage with your grief in healthy ways that will lead to hope and healing.

NOTICE CATASTROPHIZING AND OTHER COGNITIVE DISTORTIONS

For some people, anxiety in grief takes the form of fixating on worst-case scenarios. This is called catastrophizing—in other words, turning a normal concern into an imagined catastrophe.

Our minds naturally think through what-ifs and foresee possible scenarios to come. This is a necessary human cognitive skill. It's what allows us to plan and tackle everything from making lunch and doing our schoolwork to running a household and accomplishing the work our jobs require.

Catastrophizing, on the other hand, is a type of cognitive distortion. It's imagining the very worst outcomes and believing that they might well happen.

Other types of cognitive distortion that can increase anxiety are jumping to conclusions, overgeneralizing, and filtering out positives in a situation while focusing on negatives.

If your typical thought patterns are worsening your anxiety, this is a good reason to see a counselor. Counselors are trained to help you recognize your thought distortions and replace them with habits of mind that are more self-compassionate and helpful.

BECOMING AWARE OF TRIGGERS

Part of the process of learning to understand your anxiety is becoming aware of any triggers that tend to bring on or worsen your anxiety. These triggers are unique to each person and set of circumstances.

Common anxiety triggers in grief include:

• Places associated with the death

• Objects associated with the person who died

• Anniversaries, birthdays, and holidays

• Work, financial, and other concurrent life stressors

• Exhaustion

• Hunger

• Dehydration

• Physical issues

- Reminders of past life losses

- Certain sensory experiences—smells, tastes, music, etc.

- Drugs and/or alcohol

Pay attention to circumstances that tend to set off or worsen your anxiousness. When you begin to see patterns in what triggers your anxiety, you will have clues about how to soothe it.

For example, if you realize that your body feels more stressed when it's dehydrated (this is quite common, by the way), you can take the simple step of ensuring you drink more water throughout the day. Or if drinking wine in the evening causes your sleep to be more disrupted, leading to worry-filled insomnia in the middle of the night (also common), you can choose to cut back on or eliminate alcohol consumption.

However, it's also important to understand that becoming aware of your anxiety triggers does not necessarily mean avoiding them. In Part Three, we'll talk about the essential task of engaging with and actively expressing your grief anxiety. If objects associated with the person who died make you feel anxious, for instance, it will likely be helpful to you (again, depending on circumstances and with appropriate timing) to intentionally encounter these objects. Avoidance in grief almost always blocks healing and prolongs anxiety. You will find that turning toward instead of away from whatever is provoking your anxiety will actually ease your anxiety. So we'll go over ways to do that safely and in small, incremental doses.

ANXIETY'S RELATIONSHIP TO YOUR OTHER GRIEF FEELINGS

So far we've been talking about anxiety as if it existed as its own emotional silo, separate from your other grief emotions. But the reality is a bit messier. Grief anxiety is often intertwined with other grief thoughts and feelings you would probably label as something else.

For example, for some people guilt and regret are common, normal grief emotions. They are stressful, so they simultaneously tend to cause anxiety. If you are feeling guilty about something related to the death or your relationship with the person who died, you are likely to feel anxious about this guilt and/or regret.

Anger is also a close cousin to anxiety. They both arise from stress hormones. Anger is often more outward-directed, and anxiety tends to be more inward-directed, but they can both be nerve-racking, tense feelings.

You may also experience anxiety alongside or as a result of other common grief feelings, such as disorientation (causing you to feel anxious that you're not thinking clearly) and relief (causing anxiety that you shouldn't be feeling relieved), among others.

All of this is to say that anxiety in grief can be, in some ways, a feeling that blankets everything else. The suggestions in this book will help you gently pull back the blanket so you can see what else is there and work on acknowledging, understanding, and mourning all of it.

PART TWO:
SOOTHING YOUR ANXIETY

*"Almost everything will work again if you unplug
it for a few minutes, including you."*
— Anne Lamott

Whenever you need relief from your normal and necessary grief anxiety, it's time for self-care. Developing a toolkit of techniques and activities that work for you to soothe your anxiety when it's too powerful is an essential step.

The following tips and activities may help ease your stress and fears. Any time you feel overly anxious, restless, or afraid, give one of them a try. Keep testing out different approaches until you find at least a few that reliably work for you. As with everything in grief, there is no right or wrong way to do things. You are the expert of your grief. You get to decide what helps you feel safer, comforted, and more relaxed.

Keep Linking Objects Close
Linking objects are items that belonged to the person who died that you might now like to have around you. Objects

such as clothing, books, knick-knacks, jewelry, artwork, and other prized possessions can help you feel physically closer to the person you miss so much. They can also help you feel safer and calmer.

If you like to hold, be near, look at, sleep with, caress, or smell a special belonging of the person who died, you're simply trying to hold on to a tangible, physical connection to the person. The person's body is no longer physically here, but these special items are. And if they help you make it through the naturally anxiety-filled days of your grief, so much the better.

Comfort Yourself
Comfort means being at ease physically and mentally. That can seem all but impossible to achieve in grief, but in between "doses" of active mourning (see page 24), I hope you will seek relaxation and respite by caring for yourself as much as possible.

If there was ever a time to indulge yourself with your favorite comforts, it's now. In fact, think of them as survival tactics—not indulgences. Take a nap. Curl up on the sofa with your softest blanket and binge your favorite TV show. Eat your favorite comfort foods. Take a long shower or bath. Meet up with friends at your favorite restaurant, or invite a good friend over for take-out. Ask for hugs. Have someone give you a foot or neck massage. Listen to soothing music. Watch the sunset. Play a game on your phone. Play with your pet. Reread your favorite book.

You get the idea. Come up with a list of actions that help you feel comforted or soothed. Whatever those things are for you, do them often and guilt-free. However, do watch out for overusing alcohol and drugs (see page 30), and take care not to over-isolate. But, otherwise, do what soothes your body, mind, and soul.

See a Physician and/or Counselor

If you are feeling so anxious that you're having a hard time sleeping, eating, and functioning, it's a good idea to schedule a check-up with your primary-care provider. This would also be a good time to consider seeing a grief counselor for a few sessions.

I'm not suggesting there is anything wrong with you! I have simply seen time and again that getting a little professional reassurance and support for the normal, intense symptoms of grief can help you better survive and take steps to understand them.

Your medical provider can help assure you that any physical symptoms of grief you may be experiencing—heart palpitations, body aches, headaches, trouble sleeping, and more—aren't due to an illness that needs diagnosis and treatment. If you're having any physical concerns that mimic the symptoms/cause of death of the person who died—for example, if you've been having chest discomfort, and your loved one died of a heart attack—your primary-care provider can help ease your anxiety by ruling out this possibility.

Like seeing a physician, grief counseling is another basic form of self-care. Just a few sessions with a grief counselor can help you better understand and soothe your anxiety. They can also help support you while you are experiencing the pain of grief. Whatever your most hurtful, scariest thoughts and feelings are at the moment, you can share them with your counselor. In fact, openly talking about your struggles in the presence of a compassionate, grief-informed counselor may be the single most effective thing you can do to soothe your fears and other intense feelings.

I've also noticed that some people think of self-care wellness practices such as yoga, massage, and acupuncture as normal parts of routine physical, emotional, and spiritual maintenance, while other people construe them as overly indulgent or unnecessary. When it comes to caring for yourself when experiencing grief, I assure you they are not indulgent. I encourage you to give any of these wellness practices a try if they feel right for you.

Move Your Body

As we've seen, fear is a primal physical response. Moving your body is an excellent way to reduce the stress chemicals while also increasing the biochemicals that boost feelings of contentment, ease, and happiness, such as dopamine, serotonin, and endorphins.

Light exercise can do wonders for lessening anxiety and enhancing feelings of wellbeing. You can start really small if you are not physically active already. Try walking for ten minutes to start with, then gradually increase the duration. If you don't like walking, choose an activity you enjoy more, such as biking, yoga, shooting hoops, pickleball, or gardening.

Make Sleep a Priority

Good sleep and wellness go hand in hand. Poor sleep and anxiety do too.

Insomnia is often a normal part of grief. But if you're not sleeping and incapable of functioning due to exhaustion, it's probably time to get help with your sleep.

See your primary-care provider and explain your sleep challenges. Temporary use of sleep medication or supplements such as melatonin might be wise. You can also try relaxation and sleep apps on your phone, such as Calm and Loona. It is worth continuing the search until you find tools that help you get adequate sleep.

Do Breathing Exercises

Whenever you feel anxious, try turning your attention to your breath. You'll likely notice that when you're anxious, your breathing has become quick and shallow. Consciously work to make your breathing slow and deep. Breathe in deeply from your diaphragm. Put your hand on your upper belly and push out your hand as you inhale slowly through your nose then exhale slowly through pursed lips. Whenever your mind wanders from paying attention to your breath, bring your focus back to your breath. After five minutes of deep, mindful breathing, notice how your anxiety level may have changed. Some studies have shown that mindful breathing is as effective as prescription medication in treating anxiety disorders.

Tune Into Your Body

Since anxiety is felt in the body, get in the habit of tuning into your bodily sensations of anxiety. In any given moment, where are you feeling it? What does it feel like? How would you describe the sensation(s)?

Now turn your attention to a different part of your body that is not feeling anxious. Let's say your knee is neutral or comfortable. What other body parts are neutral or comfortable? Taking inventory of your body's anxiety in this way can help you teach your body that anxiety is not an all-consuming experience, that you are safe, and that you can manage it.

Visualize Calm

Close your eyes and imagine a serene place. For many people this might be a beach or a mountain meadow. Imagine you are sitting and gazing at the view. Practice mindful breathing as you visualize. Return to this place in your mind whenever you need a dose of calm and a reminder that it is possible to shape your moment-to-moment experience.

Try Meditation or Yoga

Meditation, yoga, and other mindfulness activities are good techniques to add to your soothing toolkit. Try a class, lesson, or app to help you get started. Many people find that once they learn a simple mindfulness practice that works for them, they're hooked. They feel healthier and more grounded than they ever have before. Prayer is a similar activity that calms and grounds many people.

Get Into a Routine

Daily routines help us feel more in control, and feeling more in control is a way to counteract anxiety. Try getting up at the same time each morning, eating a healthy breakfast, going for a short walk, writing in a grief journal or talking to a friend, etc.

If some part of your daily routine makes you feel anxious, try eliminating it for now. For example, maybe scrolling on social media is feeding your anxiety. If so, take a break from it for the time being.

Get Outside

When we are grieving, we need relief from our fear and pain. Today we often turn to technology for distraction when what we really need is the opposite: generous doses of nature. Studies show that time spent outdoors lowers blood pressure, eases depression and anxiety, bolsters the immune system, lessens stress, and even makes us more compassionate.

Engaging with the natural world is a tonic for soothing the anxieties of grief. It's next to impossible to feel anxious in a calm, beautiful, quiet outdoor setting. Find a few natural, nearby places where you can go to sit and relax. If you have enough energy, take a gentle walk. Notice what happens to your feelings of fear and anxiety when you spend time in your natural refuges.

Go to Other Calming Places

Also identify other nearby places that, when you're there, help you feel calm. They might include your bedroom, your couch, your bathtub, a friend's house, a church sanctuary or other place of worship. When you're feeling anxious, go to one of your calming places and spend 15 minutes there. Ask a loved one to be with you if you think it would help you to simultaneously talk about your grief.

Be Careful of Alcohol and Drug Use

Many people turn to alcohol and drugs to help them feel

less anxiety and pain after a major loss. Nobody wants to experience hurt of this magnitude. Looking to numb the pain and fear is understandable.

The problem with using drugs and alcohol to cope with grief, of course, is that they can harm our bodies and are also habit-forming. What's more, when they are relied on too often, they distance us from the reality of our loss and grief. I have seen many times that substance use hindered or complicated healing rather than helped it.

If others express concern about your alcohol or drug use, or if you yourself are wondering if the frequency and/or degree of your substance use are healthy, I urge you to talk to your primary-care provider about it. Cutting back is probably a good idea, and if you are struggling with addiction, getting help right now is the wisest, most self-compassionate thing you can do.

IF YOUR LOSS WAS TRAUMATIC

The natural stress, anxiety, and fears of early grief are typically more challenging after a traumatic death.

What may be considered a traumatic death varies. Sudden and/or violent deaths are almost always thought of as traumatic. Deaths with uncertain causes, out-of-order deaths (such as the death of a young person), and deaths that happen at the same time as other major life stressors also tend to feel traumatic.

If your loss was traumatic in some way, you may be naturally experiencing heightened fear and anxiety. Post-traumatic stress is real. I use the term "traumatic grief."

If you are experiencing traumatic grief, I urge you to see an experienced grief counselor. You may need more care to help you with heightened anxiety of traumatic grief. Your grief is still normal, but the circumstances of the loss are abnormally challenging. The extra layer of support a grief counselor will provide can make all the difference.

Spend Time with Loved Ones and Pets

I can't overstate how necessary it is when you're in grief to spend time with people (and, if you have them, pets) who care about you. You may feel like isolating yourself—closing your bedroom door, crawling into bed, and pulling the covers over your head—but too much isolation is not good for you, especially if you're anxious. Being alone with your thoughts and fears only tends to make them worse.

Studies have proven that spending time with friends and family helps us cope with stress and elevates our mood. Because it lowers cortisol levels, it also improves our cardiovascular health and boosts our immune systems, among other benefits.

The Anxiety of Grief

I'm not saying that alone time can't also be good and necessary in grief, because it is. The natural fatigue of grief makes rest and solitude a priority as well. There are times in life we all need to go to exile. But if your fears are making you feel crazy or your anxiety is so pronounced that it is difficult for you to get through the day, please—reach out to others. Texts, phone calls, and emails can support you at any time of the day or night. And whenever possible, spend time with others in person.

Talking about your fears is certainly an effective way to diminish them. The more you express and explore them, the less power they will have over you. But it also helps to simply spend time in the company of others. It's OK not to talk about your loss all the time if you don't want to or don't have the energy. Just being around friends and family is often enough to reduce anxiety and bolster feelings of wellbeing.

Allowing others to take care of you is also important. When friends and family members cook for you, clean for you, run errands for you, and take care of tasks for you, what they're really doing is expressing their love for you. They're also trying to help ensure you feel as safe and comforted as possible. If you are someone who is not used to being taken care of by others, you might need to make a conscious effort to accept their support.

Pets can also provide solace and support when we're grieving. As pet parents know, their unconditional love is such a comfort. It's hard to feel afraid when a dog is licking your face or a cat is purring in your lap. So by all means, if you're a pet person, turn to your pets for soothing whenever you get the chance.

You need other people (and companion animals, if you have them) to help you counteract your anxiety. Let them.

Start the Habit of Checking in with Yourself

My many years as a grief counselor have taught me that people are often unaware of how they're feeling. They move through life doing, but they've never learned to be present to their emotions.

If you are not doing it already, now is a good time to start the habit of checking in with yourself.

First thing each morning, last thing each night, and several times throughout each day, stop whatever it is you are doing and ask yourself, "How am I feeling right now?" Name your feeling(s) and care for yourself accordingly.

If you are feeling anxious, take steps to soothe your anxiety. I hope the ideas in this section give you a few things to try.

As you get better at recognizing your anxiety and more experienced at coping with it, your anxiety will naturally become less powerful. You'll know what works for you to help yourself survive and eventually thrive.

PART THREE:

EXPRESSING YOUR ANXIETY

*"And the time came when the risk to remain tight in a
bud was more painful than the risk it took to blossom."*

— Anais Nin

Several times in this book I've mentioned the concept of
mourning your grief. Now it's time to focus on that.

Mourning means expressing your grief outside of yourself. It's
dipping into your inner grief—all the thoughts and feelings
in your grief basket—and taking them out of the basket to
present them to the world in some way.

Whenever a thought or feeling is strong and keeps grabbing
your attention, that means you need to mourn it.

The idea is to keep mourning one day at a time for as long as
it takes for the thoughts and feelings in your grief basket to
soften. As you continue to openly and fully mourn them, they
will begin to fade, much as vibrant, fresh flowers eventually
become dried flowers. Your grief will never disappear
completely. It will always be there, but if you do the work of

grief, if you mourn well, it will fade into the background and become an integrated, bittersweet piece of the story of your entire life.

Like sadness, anger, guilt, and other grief feelings, your anxiety is part of your grief, so it also needs to be mourned. You mourn your fears and anxieties by acknowledging and sharing them.

But wait a minute. Can't you just think about and feel your grief inside of you? Isn't that enough? The answer is no. Anxiety, especially, thrives on secrecy and seclusion. It likes to grow in the dark. But the more you expose it to the light of day, the more you typically find that it's not nearly as big and terrible as it made itself out to be.

Here are some common, effective ways of mourning your anxiety:

- *Crying*
  By all means, cry whenever you feel like it. Crying releases stress chemicals in your tears. Notice how much calmer you may feel after a good cry.

- *Talking to a good listener*
  Expressing your fears and anxieties to someone who will listen without judging or giving advice (unless you ask for advice) is one of the best ways to mourn and diffuse your anxiety.

- *Writing in a grief journal*

  Not everyone enjoys writing, but even if you don't consider yourself a writer, I urge you to give this a try. It's not at all about "good writing." Instead, it's about attempting to put words to your thoughts and feelings. Naming and describing emotions and experiences in writing helps tame and transform them.

- *Writing in other forms*

  Sharing your anxieties in texts and emails to friends can also be an effective practice. Ask a close friend for permission to text them whenever you're feeling especially anxious. They don't need to "solve" your anxiety, though. They don't need to give advice or tell you what to do (unless you ask for this). Instead, suggest that you simply need them to read the texts and perhaps respond with a simple "I hear you" or a hug emoji. As with all types of mourning, you'll find that the healing is in the expression itself, one day at a time.

- *Expending the energy*

  Anxiety is a naturally tense feeling. It builds nervous energy and stress chemicals inside you. When you release that energy in some way, you feel calmer. Physical activity is one way. We talked about the effectiveness of moving your body on page 27. Other ideas for expending energy include immersing yourself in any activity that absorbs you, helping someone else, getting a massage, making art, or going for a drive.

DOSING FEAR AND ANXIETY

One of the main principles of healing in grief is that grief and mourning can only be encountered in doses. We've already discussed the dangers of living in constant anxiety. It's not good for our bodies or souls. But if you're experiencing grief anxiety, you can and should safely engage with it in short, intermittent stints. This is also true of your other grief symptoms.

Let's say you've realized you're afraid that something bad is going to happen as a result of the death. Maybe there's something particular you are apprehensive about. You've been worrying about this potential outcome. Perhaps you've been avoiding doing anything about it or giving attention to it.

To dose yourself with that aspect of your anxiety, you're going to face it in safe, small ways, one step at a time. Perhaps you'll start by telling someone else about it—sharing your fears aloud to one other person you know to be an empathetic listener. Maybe next, on a different day, you'll investigate the facts of the fear a little. You'll learn more about the reality versus your imagined reality. Later, on yet another day, perhaps you'll write an email or note to someone expressing that fear. Or maybe you'll gather up a couple of people who are involved (or who are simply good sounding boards) and ask them for their advice and compassionate support. You'll solicit help.

This is how you dose the expression of fear and anxiety. In brief, periodic sessions. Then in between, you give yourself permission to rest, soothe yourself, and avoid the anxiety-causing concern.

The magic of dosing fear and anxiety is that it diminishes the power of whatever it is you're worried about. Psychologists call it exposure therapy. Studies have proven that safely and intentionally encountering feared circumstances reduces fear and decreases avoidance. The exposure to the feared object or situation can be done in real life, or it can be imagined or role played.

Dosing yourself with your fears and anxieties helps you realize that they are not as powerful as you imagined them to be. You also get used to them. They become more "normal" and less strange. You learn that you are a capable person, able to face your fears and survive. And you learn that fear itself, while normal, needn't be that scary.

Franklin Delano Roosevelt famously said, "The only thing we have to fear is fear itself." I would adjust this by saying that the only thing we have to fear is fear that is denied, avoided, suppressed, and unexpressed. Because fear itself is normal, and when it is acknowledged and expressed as it arises, one day at a time, it naturally becomes less fearsome and more manageable.

TELLING YOUR STORY OF LOVE AND LOSS

One of the most effective ways you can mourn the death and in doing so alleviate your fears and anxieties is to tell your story of love and loss. It really is that simple.

Your story of love and loss contains all the details and complexities of who you are, who the person who died was, what your relationship was like, how you spent time together, who the other people in your shared story were, where you lived, all the memories big and small, good and bad, as well as the story of the death itself. In other words, your story of love and loss is a tapestry.

I often remind mourners that they have to go backward before they can go forward. The more you tell the story, the more your mind and soul are able to make sense of and integrate everything that happened along the way—including the death. In telling the story over and over again, you're teaching yourself the narrative. You're creating pathways in your brain that help it come to terms with what happened. I have seen that panic attacks, especially, are often an indicator that a griever needs to reflect back on an earlier, loss-related threat to their sense of safety and security.

You can tell your story by talking to a friend who's a good listener, by writing it down in a journal, by participating in a grief support group (in person or online), by doing grief rituals, by making art about it, and by seeing a counselor.

TELLING THE STORY TO A SUPPORT GROUP

Grief support groups can do wonders to relieve your anxiety. Whatever you're afraid of, you're likely to find that other support group participants share your fears. Seeing that anxieties that come with grief are normal makes them much less scary.

Think of grief support groups as places where fellow journeyers gather and anxieties fall away, if only for an hour or two. Each of you has a story to tell, and each of you can be a good listener and supporter of others. Lifelong friends are often made in support groups, and these friendships can help sustain you as well as enrich your life.

If you think a support group might be of help to you, consider reaching out to local hospices, funeral homes, faith groups, and other agencies. They often retain lists of support groups available in your community.

TELLING THE STORY TO A GRIEF COUNSELOR

Individual counseling is an excellent addition to any griever's self-care plan. A good grief counselor will help you feel seen, heard, affirmed, and understood as you share the many facets of your grief—including your anxiety. In fact, you can think of the grief counselor's office as a safe space in which to relieve your anxiety. If you have found a skilled, compassionate grief counselor, you may arrive at your sessions feeling tense and keyed up, but you will often leave feeling a sense of relief and release.

ACTIVELY EXPLORING MEMORIES

Actively exploring memories that took place throughout the entire timeline of the person's life as well as your relationship with them is one essential way of mourning. This allows you to remember the story so that you can ponder it and retell it to yourself and others.

But does the idea of actively exploring memories make you feel anxious? If so, that's a sign that this is an area of mourning you need to work on. Over time, your avoidance will begin to make the anxiety worse. I understand that remembering can hurt. But what I have seen in my decades as a grief counselor is that any prolonged anxiety about the idea of remembering is typically worse than the pain of actively remembering. Active remembering helps your mind and soul begin to come to terms with the death. It also helps you feel and express your ongoing love for the person who died.

When you're ready, make time to encounter your memories in doses. Set aside half an hour here or an hour there to look through photos and videos. At some point, you may find that putting together photo books and memory boxes is a transformative activity. Going through the person's belongings is another facet of remembering. Writing down anecdotes and biographical information is also an excellent way to explore memories.

SCHEDULING EXPRESSION INTO YOUR DAY

I've noticed that some people avoid mourning because it seems like an overwhelming task. The grief is always there, so does that mean you need to be mourning all the time? And as I've said, this avoidance tends to amplify grief anxiety.

We've already reviewed the concept of dosing grief and mourning (page 38). It's critical to think of actively engaging with your grief as something to be done in short stints, with lots of time for rest and distraction in between. But in addition to dosing your grief as it naturally arises in you, you can also carve out intentional pockets of time for mourning in your schedule.

For example, what if you were to set aside 15 minutes or half an hour for active mourning each day? Let's say you choose a time in the morning. Every day at 9 a.m., you work on expressing your grief in some simple way. This doesn't mean that your grief won't naturally come up whenever it feels like it, but it does mean that you've already made an agreement with it: I may not have the time or energy to engage with you right now, but I promise that I will tomorrow morning at 9 a.m. If you follow through (and keep up with it for as long as you need to), this practice, in turn, will almost certainly reduce your grief anxiety over time because you will be giving it regular time and attention.

EXPRESSING THROUGH MOURNING RITUALS

Grief rituals can help you express and tame your anxiety.

What do I mean by grief rituals? I simply mean actions that we perform in a certain way and in a certain sequence. We perform them for a purpose that has emotional and spiritual meaning and is greater than the sum of its parts. Rituals don't have to be formal ceremonies, though. In fact, most of them can be brief, informal, and simple.

The ingredients of grief rituals are:

Intentionality
Take a few seconds at the beginning of each ritual to speak your intention. In other words, state what you intend to gain or reinforce from the activity. For example, "the purpose of this ritual is to honor and remember what _____ brought to my life."

Actions
Rituals always involve your body. Moving or using your body in certain ways as you perform a ritual helps integrate your

physical, cognitive, emotional, social, and spiritual selves. Examples include lighting a candle, holding your body in a certain posture, bowing your head, standing in a certain spot, moving from point A to point B to point C, etc.

Symbolism

Symbols are significant elements of ritual. Objects important to your story of loss and ongoing love can be powerful touchstones in your grief rituals. These are often linking objects but can also be spiritual symbols, flowers, candles, and more.

Sequence

Rituals have a beginning, middle, and end. The parts of the ritual are usually performed in a certain order because the sequence itself builds meaning and effectiveness.

Presence

Rituals stand apart from the rest of our days. We don't allow the busy-ness of our lives to intrude on them. Instead, we create a time and place, and we commit to being fully present as we carry out the ritual.

Heart

Rituals are emotional. In performing grief rituals, we commit to being open to and accepting of whatever emotions arise. We allow ourselves the gift of time and presence to acknowledge, welcome, and feel our feelings, no matter what they are.

Spirit

The spiritual nature of ritual is what creates the transformative power of the experience. On the surface, we may seem to be carrying out a series of simple, no-big-deal actions. But with the addition of intention, symbolism, sequence, presence, and heart, we are elevating the experience into the realm of the spiritual.

You can combine these seven elements in a million ways to create simple, brief grief rituals to incorporate into your daily life.

One example is what I call the "Ten-Minute Grief Encounter Ritual." Here's how it works:

- First, find a quiet space and center yourself.

- Then set your intention for the ritual on that day. If you're working on inventorying and expressing your anxiety, it might be to feel calmer.

- Then, while holding or looking at a symbol of the person who died (such as a photo or article of clothing), name the anxieties you are having and acknowledge their normalcy. You might say something like, "I am feeling anxious that _____. Such fears are a natural part of grief."

- As you name each new thought and feeling, place your free hand over your heart, pressing gently, then allow your hand to fall to a resting position again.

The Anxiety of Grief

- If you are someone who prays, you can pray these thoughts and feelings instead as you step through the ritual.

- Continue feeling, naming, and exploring your anxieties for five to ten minutes. When the time is up, take a moment to express your gratitude for anything authentic you thought, felt, and acknowledged during the ritual.

- Close with an affirmation that restates the intention you set at the beginning of the ritual but this time as a present truth. For example, "I am fearful in my grief, but I can express my fears and in doing so, help alleviate them."

Now that you know what I mean by a simple daily grief ritual, I'm sure you can come up with ideas of your own. If you need more ideas, my book *Grief Day by Day: Simple Everyday Practices to Help Yourself Survive…and Thrive* contains numerous examples.

The amazing thing about grief rituals is that they naturally facilitate healing. This is especially true when they're done regularly, day in and day out. For anxiety in particular, rituals help your mind and heart feel a little more in control. You may not be able to control life and death (none of us can!), but you can control the intentionality, symbolism, sequence, etc. of this grief ritual.

I urge you to give grief rituals a try as you work on finding ways to express your anxiety. I have seen them work effectively many times in the lives and hearts of grieving people. In fact, ritual is so effective in grief that when I meet a griever who is especially struggling, I often recommend additional rituals in addition to or in lieu of talk therapy.

THE IMPORTANCE OF CONGRUENCE

Psychologists talk about a concept they call "congruence." Congruence means that your outer words and behaviors align with your inner feelings and thoughts. The outside matches the inside.

Congruence is essential because it feels right. It's truthful and genuine. Incongruence, on the other hand, feels wrong. It's withholding and dishonest. And it actually compounds anxiety.

When it comes to mourning your anxiety, only honesty works. It can take courage to be fully honest about your worries and fears, to be vulnerable enough to show others what's inside you. But here I encourage you to understand the importance of being authentic with your grief and mourning.

Your true, raw grief anxiety is not shameful. Any shame you might feel about authentically mourning it is often a result of unhealthy cultural taboos and stigmas. So whatever your feelings and thoughts are on the inside, they need authentic representation on the outside. They need you to give them full, accurate, honest voice.

If you are reticent to mourn your anxiety (or any grief thought or feeling) fully and authentically, consider starting by writing down your thoughts and feelings. This is a more private, safer method of mourning. Also try talking to your most empathetic, nonjudgmental friend. Tell them one anxious thought you've been afraid to express aloud, then see how they respond. Usually mourners find that any thoughts and feelings they've been holding back for fear of sounding abnormal or foolish are not only understood, they are frequently shared by others.

There is nothing wrong with you, and there is nothing wrong with your grief. Again, strive to express your anxiety authentically. Whatever you are feeling and thinking, mourn it honestly and fully. It's the only way to heal and truly live and love each precious remaining day of your life.

A FINAL WORD

*"Anxiety isn't you. It's something moving through you.
It can leave out of the same door it came in."*
— James Clear

Your grief isn't you. It's something moving through you.

Your anxiety isn't you. It's something moving through you.

In order to give your grief and anxiety movement, though, you must express them openly, honestly, and fully. Mourning is what gives your grief and anxiety momentum toward healing.

In grief, healing is reconciliation. It is a place in which you have fully acknowledged the reality of the death and integrated that reality into your ongoing life. The sharp, ever-present pain of grief gives rise to a renewed sense of meaning and purpose. Your grief symptoms, including your anxiety, soften, and you are once again interested and involved in the activities of living.

Usually there is not one great moment of "arrival" at reconciliation. Instead, there is a series of subtle changes and incremental progress. While you may well experience setbacks along the way, in general there is a forward motion that is fueled by active mourning and the desire to meaningfully live out the rest of your precious remaining days.

On the journey, I hope you work hard to understand and soothe your anxiety, mourn well, cultivate hope, connect with others, and rediscover meaning and purpose.

I hope we meet one day.

ABOUT THE AUTHOR

Alan D. Wolfelt, Ph.D., is a respected author and educator on the topics of companioning others and healing in grief. He serves as Director of the Center for Loss and Life Transition and is on the faculty at the University of Colorado Medical

 School's Department of Family Medicine. Dr. Wolfelt has written many bestselling books on healing in grief, including *Understanding Your Grief, Healing Your Grieving Heart*, and *Grief One Day at a Time*. Visit www.centerforloss.com to learn more about grief and loss and to order Dr. Wolfelt's books.

The Hope and Healing Series
Concise books of wisdom and comfort

Readers and counselors often ask Dr. Wolfelt to write books on specialized topics not well-covered elsewhere in the grief literature. He created the Hope and Healing Series to fulfill their requests. These short books focus in on particular types of loss and aspects of grief that while distinct, are not uncommon. They affect many millions of people worldwide, each of whom deserves affirmation, support, and guidance for their unique circumstances.

All Dr. Wolfelt's publications can be ordered by mail from:
Companion Press, 3735 Broken Bow Road, Fort Collins, CO 80526
(970) 226-6050 • www.centerforloss.com

First Aid for Broken Hearts

Life is both wonderful and devastating. It graces us with joy, and

it breaks our hearts. If your heart is broken, this book is for you.

Loss may be an unavoidable part of human life, but it doesn't have to prevent you from living well. You can and will survive this. Actually, if you adopt this guide's basic principles, revealed and tested by Dr. Wolfelt, you will even go on to thrive.

ISBN 978-1-61722-281-8
118 pages • softcover • $9.95

All Dr. Wolfelt's publications can be ordered by mail from:
Companion Press, 3735 Broken Bow Road, Fort Collins, CO 80526
(970) 226-6050 • www.centerforloss.com

Understanding Your Grief [SECOND EDITION]

This book is Dr. Wolfelt's most comprehensive, covering the essential lessons that mourners have taught him in his four decades of

working with the bereaved. In compassionate, down-to-earth language, *Understanding Your Grief* describes ten touchstones—or trail markers—that are essential physical, emotional, cognitive, social, and spiritual signs for mourners to look for on their journey through grief.

Think of your grief as a wilderness—a vast, inhospitable forest. You must journey through this wilderness. In the wilderness of your grief, the touchstones are your trail markers. They are the signs that let you know you are on the right path. When you learn to identify and rely on the touchstones, you will find your way to hope and healing.

ISBN 978-1-617223-07-5 • 240 pages • softcover • $14.95

All Dr. Wolfelt's publications can be ordered by mail from:
Companion Press, 3735 Broken Bow Road, Fort Collins, CO 80526
(970) 226-6050 • www.centerforloss.com

YOUR NOTES ON THE ANXIETY OF GRIEF

_____

_____

_____

_____

_____

_____

_____

_____

_____

_____

_____

_____

_____

_____

_____

_____

_____

_____

_____

_____

YOUR NOTES ON THE ANXIETY OF GRIEF

_____

_____

_____

_____

_____

_____

_____

_____

_____

_____

_____

_____

_____

_____

_____

_____

_____

_____

_____

_____

_____

_____

_____

YOUR NOTES ON THE ANXIETY OF GRIEF

_____

_____

_____

_____

_____

_____

_____

_____

_____

_____

_____

_____

_____

_____

_____

_____

_____

_____

_____

_____

_____

_____